7 Essentials for Character Discipline

7 Essentials for Character Discipline

Elementary Classroom Management

Sandra P. Davis-Johnson

CORWIN PRESS, INC.
A SAGE PUBLICATIONS COMPANY
Thousand Oaks, CA 91320-2218

For information:

Corwin Press, Inc.
A Sage Publications Company
2455 Teller Road
Thousand Oaks, California 91320
E-mail: order@corwinpress.com

CORWIN
PRESS

Sage Publications Ltd.
6 Bonhill Street
London EC2A 4PU
United Kingdom

Sage Publications India Pvt. Ltd.
M-32 Market
Greater Kailash I
New Delhi 110 048 India

Library of Congress Cataloging-in-Publication Data

Davis-Johnson, Sandra P.
  Seven essentials for character discipline: Elementary
classroom management / by Sandra P. Davis-Johnson.
     p. cm.
  ISBN 0-7619-7642-6 (cloth: alk. paper)
  ISBN 0-7619-7643-4 (pbk.: alk. paper)
  1. Classroom management—United States. 2. Character—Study
and teaching (Elementary)—United States. 3. Moral education
(Elementary)—United States. I. Title: 7 essentials for character
discipline. II. Title.
  LB3013.039 2000
  372.1102′4—dc21   00-008748

This book is printed on acid-free paper.

01 02 03 04 05 10 9 8 7 6 5 4 3 2 1

Corwin Editorial Assistant: Julia Parnell
Production Editor: Nevair Kabakian
Editorial Assistant: Candice Crosetti
Typesetter/Designer: Janelle LeMaster

Contents

Preface

The primary purpose of writing down my systematic classroom management program is to share and provide an alternative and positive method of developing an environment conducive to academic learning and success. In my 17 years as a classroom teacher of both elementary and high school students, I have discovered that Essential Character Discipline allows the educator to establish a learning atmosphere of self-respect, perseverance, and self-control. By modeling these characteristics daily, the classroom teacher provides opportunities for students to develop and practice these positive behaviors that lead to academic success. Too many students go to school for the wrong reasons and are not self-motivated to strive for academic excellence. Essential Character Discipline provides a systematic management approach for classroom teachers, using the Essential Character Discipline Vocabulary as a foundation for positive classroom behavior by teachers and students.

> Once students realize that positive classroom behavior and academic success go hand in hand, then the learning environment becomes a place of production.

Essential Character Discipline is a product of my professional efforts in working directly with elementary and high school students. This management system resulted primarily from my exposure to and observation of negative behavior patterns of children. As I observed more and more students in the classroom, I became aware that a large majority of students lacked respect for self and others. I also noticed that teachers were not always modeling positive behaviors in their classrooms. As a result of these observations, I decided to put into print my general classroom management system. Once students realize that positive classroom behavior and academic success go hand in hand, then the learning environment becomes a place of production. Essential Character Discipline is a systematic approach designed to help individuals learn the important elements of integrity that develop an environment conducive to academic learning and success.

> Teach children to honor themselves and others, and they will tell the truth. If they tell the truth, they will respect themselves. If they respect themselves, they will be concerned for others. If they are concerned for others, they will exhibit positive behaviors in school that will contribute to a learning environment of success and academic achievement.

Essential Character Discipline seeks to expose students to the meanings of the Essential Character Discipline Vocabulary on a daily basis, to provide students with a model of positive behavior, and to develop classroom environments that encourage academic success. The overall aim of Essential Character Discipline is to provide positive educational environments, develop the self-esteem and positive self-concepts of students, develop the students' respect for self and others, and emphasize the importance of academic achievement.

Students who are grounded in the essential characteristics of courtesy, loyalty, respect, perseverance, honor, integrity, and self-control will be successful and self-motivated in the world of academics. Teach children to honor themselves and others, and they will tell the truth. If they tell the truth, they will respect themselves. If they respect themselves, they will be concerned for others. If they are concerned for others, they will exhibit positive behaviors in school that will contribute to a learning environment of success and academic achievement. Essential Character Discipline enables the teacher to provide a positive classroom setting that leads to productivity, academic success, and learning.

Children need the security of knowing procedures, expectations, and limits. They need to know that class expectations will be high and required. The educational environment that fosters courtesy and respect leads to academic success. The classroom that encourages loyalty and perseverance leads to academic achievement. The academic setting that models integrity and self-control leads to high self-esteem and academic attainment.

Chapter 1 provides the teacher with the rationale, instructional program, and behavioral objectives of Essential Character Discipline. Through exposure to and understanding of the Essential Character Discipline Vocabulary via the model of positive behaviors by the teacher, the students' educational environment leads to productivity, academic success, and learning. The teacher who models the behaviors of positive self-concepts, self-confidence, and respect for others and who establishes the importance of academic achievement also realizes the value of communication with parents, parental support, and parental participation in positive classroom behavior and academic success. Teachers should use a variety of teaching methods to meet the individual learning styles of students. The receptive or input learning process (visual and tactile perceptions) and the expressive or output learning process (verbal and visual-motor expressions) are addressed in Essential Character Discipline to develop positive behaviors that will lead to respect for self and others and to academic success.

On completion of Essential Character Discipline, the students will (a) understand the Essential Character Discipline Vocabulary (*courtesy, loyalty, respect, perseverance, honor, integrity,* and *self-control*); (b) voluntarily participate in and model positive classroom behavior; (c) develop a work ethic that leads to academic success; (d) have self-control of actions; (e) orally

> When students show respect for self and others, the positive behaviors necessary for academic success are plentiful in the learning environment.

state the Student Pledge; and (f) keep the lines of communication open between parents and the school. The communication of the goal and aim of Essential Character Discipline to parents or guardians establishes a working relationship that makes them aware of the relationship between positive classroom behaviors and academic success.

In Chapter 2, the individual components of Essential Character Discipline are described in detail: positive verbal communication, modeling of positive behaviors, and the establishment of limits and expectations. These components will help the teacher enforce classroom rules. The teacher is a powerful figure in the lives of each student. Essential Character Discipline is the necessary distinguishing feature of obedience to authority. This chapter lists the rights of the educator and the rights of the students and introduces and defines the Essential Character Discipline Vocabulary.

Chapter 3 tells how to get started the first day of school with Essential Character Discipline. The teacher needs to orally and visually communicate Essential Character Discipline with positive behaviors, the Essential Character Discipline Vocabulary, the Student Pledge/Contract, and the classroom rules and consequences. This chapter also lists the rights and responsibilities of parents and guardians and the positive aspects of communicating with parents. Academic success depends on the amount of support and assistance received from parents and guardians.

Chapter 4 provides the fundamentals of establishing Essential Character Discipline. The classroom teacher sets the tone of positive behavior to assist the students in reducing negative behaviors. To establish a supportive classroom, the teacher should (a) express expectations, (b) establish eye contact, (c) use nonthreatening gestures, (d) personalize messages, and (e) provide warmth and support. Daily examples of positive behaviors by the classroom teacher are vital to the success of Essential Character Discipline. The backbone of this management program is establishing and following through with consequences. If parents/guardians and teachers work together to model and reinforce the positive aspects of Essential Character Discipline and follow through with consequences for negative behaviors, students learn to be responsible for their own behavior.

Chapter 5 gives examples of how Essential Character Discipline can be used to modify the common negative behaviors of anxiety, need for approval, dependence needs, and independence seeking. Essential Character Discipline provides an environment that encourages students to live within their limits. Boundaries are established that allow students to be responsible for their behaviors. The environment helps students see that positive behaviors are in their best interest. Negative behaviors are not encouraged in an Essential Character Discipline classroom. Essential Character Discipline teachers model and reinforce behaviors that demonstrate and encourage responsibility for actions. Instead of being implemented after students have engaged in negative behaviors, Essential Character Discipline is a daily classroom management program that develops stronger self-images in students on a continual basis.

Chapter 6 addresses how the positive aspects of Essential Character Discipline can provide a successful learning environment for children who are depressed and for children who exhibit dishonest behaviors. Essential Character Discipline provides an environment free of lingering feelings of stress and tension that may contribute to depression. The teacher shows concern and consideration for the feelings of all students. In too many classrooms, children are given the message that deceitful behavior is okay because there are no established guidelines. That is not the case with the Essential Character Discipline classroom. The primary goal of Essential Character Discipline is to expose students to positive behaviors. The Essential Character Discipline classroom provides a structured environment, positive role models, and opportunities for academic success for all students in the class.

Chapter 7 reinforces the consequences for positive behaviors. The basic principle of Essential Character Discipline is to model positive behaviors of respect, courtesy, and integrity. Positive behaviors of students should always be rewarded with positive verbal responses. All students seek structure and recognition. Showing students that the teacher is truly interested in their behavior and academic success will reduce the time spent addressing negative behaviors.

The resource section contains seven parts. The glossary (Resource A) provides an alphabetical listing of appropriate vocabulary to be used on a daily basis to provide a model of positive behaviors and to develop classroom environments that encourage academic success. Suggested vocabulary activities (Resource B) are included to incorporate the glossary words in language expression, artistic expression, and cooperative learning activities. Activities are provided to address the different learning styles of practice, exploration, production, and life experience (Resource C). Key elements of Essential Character Discipline (Resource D) are listed individually, followed by the Student Pledge/Contract (Resource E), sample parent/guardian letter (Resource F), and sample award certificates (Resource G) for easy reference.

A positive classroom setting leads to productivity, comprehension, and academic success. The Essential Character Discipline classroom provides a learning environment that encourages respect for self, others, and academic achievement. Essential Character Discipline provides the teacher with the tools required to develop positive behaviors that build the self-esteem students need to establish responsibility for actions and behaviors.

The focus of Essential Character Discipline is on seven general positive behaviors: courtesy, loyalty, respect, perseverance, honor, integrity, and self-control. When students show respect for self and others, the positive behaviors necessary for academic success are plentiful in the learning environment. Students need and seek structure in the classroom. The effectiveness of Essential Character Discipline may vary with students because of age, cultural background, or parental involvement. With teachers modeling and encouraging compassion, reliability, self-esteem, courage, trust, honor, and self-control, students will be exposed to positive behaviors that inspire them to reach their fullest potential.

ACKNOWLEDGMENTS

The contributions of the following reviewers are gratefully acknowledged:

Genét Kozik-Rosabal
School of Education at the University of Colorado
Boulder, CO

Larry Krengel, Teacher
York Community High Scool
Elmhurst, IL

Courtney E. Krier, Principal
St. Felicissimus TRC School
Modesto, CA

Paula M. Lee, Third Grade Teacher
Anoka-Hennepin School District
Brooklyn Park, MN

—Sandra P. Davis-Johnson

About the Author

.

Sandra P. Davis-Johnson is a 17-year veteran teacher of exceptional children. Currently, she is the Community-Based Instruction Supervisor and classroom teacher of students who are mildly intellectually disabled and learning disabled at Southeast High School in Macon, Georgia. She received her master of education degree in interrelated studies from Mercer University in Macon and her bachelor of science degree in the field of mental retardation from Georgia College and State University in Milledgeville. She has 10 years of elementary school teaching experience with students in grades K-5. She is a member of the Middle Georgia Chapter of Phi Delta Kappa and is the proud mother of Mykel Christopher Johnson.

1

Rationale

The goal of Essential Character Discipline is to expose students to the meanings of the Essential Character Discipline Vocabulary on a daily basis, provide students with a model of positive behavior, and develop classroom environments that encourage academic success.

INSTRUCTIONAL PROGRAM

Instructional Philosophy

The overall aim of Essential Character Discipline is to provide positive educational environments, develop the self-esteem and positive self-concepts of students, develop students' respect for self and others, and emphasize the importance of academic success.

> Communicating with parents is vital in the success of Essential Character Discipline and academic achievement.

Responsibilities of the Teacher

The role of the teacher is to model behaviors of positive self-concepts, self-confidence, and respect for others and to establish the importance of academic achievement.

Communicating With Parents and Guardians

Communicating with parents and guardians is vital in the success of Essential Character Discipline and academic achievement. Parental support and participation greatly affect the success of the program. Parents and guardians need to be made aware of the relationship between positive classroom behaviors and academic attainment.

Methodological Issues

Teachers should use a variety of teaching strategies to meet the learning styles of their students. The most effective learning style for some students may be visual, whereas other students may learn more effectively through tactile or auditory modalities. By using an assortment of techniques, teachers can accommodate individual differences in learning. A student may learn best through any one of a combination of learning processes. The receptive (input) learning process includes the following:

Auditory perception: the processing and understanding of sounds and words; the assignment of meaning to words

Visual perception: the identification, organization, and interpretation of materials seen

Tactile perception: the interpretation and understanding of materials through touch

The expressive (output) process includes the following:

Verbal expression: expression of ideas and concepts through speaking

Visual-motor expression: the physical expression of material through drawing or writing

Through the various learning processes, teachers help students develop many skills:

Social/emotional skills: expressing feelings and interacting with others, including expressing and controlling feelings, cooperating with others, showing social awareness, developing self-concepts, and developing relationships with parents and relationships with adults in general

Language skills: developing communication capabilities such as listening, following directions, memory, self-expression, and reading

Cognitive skills: acquiring and using information, involving thinking, learning information, memory, imagination, problem solving, and understanding

Motor skills: using the body with control and efficiency; fine motor and gross motor mastery

Hygiene/self-help: caring for personal needs in healthy ways; recognizing needs, accepting responsibility for satisfying needs, and being able to take care of self in generally safe and accepted ways

All methodological issues are addressed in Essential Character Discipline to establish and develop positive behaviors that will lead to respect for self and others and to academic success.

Behavioral Objectives

On completion of Essential Character Discipline, students will

1. Understand the meaning of the Essential Character Discipline Vocabulary (*courtesy, loyalty, respect, perseverance, honor, integrity,* and *self-control*)

2. Voluntarily participate in and model positive classroom behavior

3. Develop a work ethic that leads to academic success

4. Have self-control of actions

5. Orally state the Student Pledge

6. Keep the lines of communication open between parents / guardians and school

2

Essential
Character Discipline

WHAT IS ESSENTIAL CHARACTER DISCIPLINE?

Essential is an adjective that means the most important properties of a thing that make it what it is. *Character* is a noun that means a distinguishing feature. *Discipline* is a noun that means training intended to elicit a specific pattern of behavior or character that results from training and is based on obedience to authority. *Essential Character Discipline* is the

> Essential Character Discipline is the necessary distinguishing feature of obedience to authority.

necessary distinguishing feature of obedience to authority. Essential Character Discipline is training that encourages the important elements of integrity. How will having Essential Character Discipline influence the behavior of students? Integrity is an indispensable element that elicits order based on obedience to authority. When students respect self and others, the needs of all students can be met. When the needs of all students are met, an environment of academic success is fostered. When limits and expectations are established, self-control, perseverance, courtesy, loyalty, and respect ensure a positive educational environment.

The teacher is in the position to influence the behavior of children in a positive way. Essential Character Discipline allows the teacher to

Rights of an Educator

The teacher has the right to

1. Establish a classroom environment that encourages respect for self and others
2. Encourage students to have self-control of their actions to be aware of the wants and needs of self and others
3. Ask for help from parents and administration in establishing Essential Character Discipline

Rights of Students

Each student has the right to

1. Learn in an environment that encourages respect and control
2. Have a teacher who will model and encourage behaviors of self-control and respect of self and others
3. Ask for help from parents or guardians, teachers, and administrators in developing Essential Character Discipline

create an environment in which students are concerned for the well-being of self, peers, and teachers. The teacher is still a powerful figure and influence in the lives of students.

The basic foundation of educational ideas of discipline has changed along with the philosophy of education. With many discipline methods, the teacher's expectations of children vary with the teacher's wants and needs. What are your rights as a classroom teacher? What do you want from your students? If you want to establish Essential Character Discipline, you need to analyze the exact behaviors you require from your students to provide a successful academic learning environment. Consider the following list of exact behaviors:

Follow directions
Raise hand to speak
Take turns
No use of profanity
Keep room clean
No fighting
No stealing
Be polite
Self-control
Tell the truth
Don't destroy property
Be on time
Have school supplies
Have assignments
Share with others
No screaming
Do your best
Respect others

Children need the security of knowing the procedures, expectations, and limits. They need to know that class expectations will be high and required. The educational environment that fosters courtesy and respect leads to academic success. The classroom that encourages loyalty and perseverance leads to academic achievement. The academic setting that models integrity and self-control leads to high self-esteem and academic attainment.

To meet these needs of students, the teacher must be a positive influence. Without positive influence and examples, students are not guaranteed an environment that encourages learning, self-respect, perseverance, and self-control. To have a positive successful classroom, it is necessary to determine the exact behaviors needed for students to reach their fullest academic potential. When establishing classroom rules, select five general behaviors. Once these rules have been determined, print and verbally present them to the students. The seven words of the Essential Character Discipline Vocabulary should be the foundation for the establishment of classroom rules (*courtesy, loyalty, respect, perseverance, honor, integrity,* and *self-control*).

To assist in determining the exact behaviors needed to establish classroom rules, answer the following questions:

1. Do you verbally communicate positive behaviors?
2. Do you model positive behaviors?
3. Have you established limits and expectations?

VERBAL COMMUNICATION

The communication of positive behaviors in the classroom by the teacher provides the students with verbal examples of Essential Character Discipline in a supportive educational setting. Examples of verbal communications for each of the seven words in the Essential Character Discipline Vocabulary are listed below.

Essential Character Discipline Vocabulary

1. *Courtesy* is a polite, helpful, or considerate act.
2. *Loyalty* is faithfulness to an idea or person.
3. *Respect* is feeling or showing honor.
4. *Perseverance* is the act of continuing.
5. *Honor* is something done or given for good behavior.
6. *Integrity* is honesty and sincerity.
7. *Self-control* is the regulation of one's emotions and actions.

Courtesy

Good morning.
Thank you.
Yes.
No.
Please excuse me.
Let's remember to stay in line.
Let's take turns.

Loyalty

We will work together to have a successful year.
You are my number one priority.
Your academic success is very important to me.

Respect

I respect your opinion, but we must all follow the rules and do the right thing.
I appreciate the way you handled yourself in that situation.

Perseverance

Although you seem to be having a hard time with this concept, we will continue to work on it until you understand.

Honor

Congratulations for modeling positive classroom behaviors.

MODELING POSITIVE BEHAVIORS

For Essential Character Discipline to be successful, the teacher must set a positive example throughout the entire day. Students need nurturing and attention to grow physically, emotionally, and academically. The teacher should provide daily examples of the Essential Character Discipline Vocabulary.

1. Courtesy
- When speaking to all students, use polite remarks or gestures.
- Never use sarcasm, jokes, or put-downs.

2. Loyalty
- At all times, remain loyal and faithful to students and the principles of Essential Character Discipline.
- Always be supportive and understanding of students' wants and needs.
- The students should always know that their academic success is your number one priority.

3. Respect
- Show concern for the feelings of all students.
- Always use polite expressions of consideration when listening to the ideas and opinions of students.

4. Perseverance
- On a daily basis, model perseverance in he completion of assignments, tasks, and activities.

- Instill in the students the importance of staying with a task until it is completed.
- Never give up on a student or on a goal for a student.

5. Honor

- Show honor for students by respecting their individual learning styles.
- Hold each student in high esteem and have high expectations for all students.

6. Integrity

- Always be honest with the students about the consequences of positive and negative behaviors.
- Always tell the truth when speaking to students on any subject.
- Set the type of example that will make the students feel that the teacher and students are one unit and that teacher and students depend on each other for positive behaviors and academic success.

7. Self-Control

- As the adult, authority figure in the classroom, always maintain self-control.
- Never use physical force.
- Never yell at a student.
- Never belittle a student.
- When you allow yourself to be pushed to the limit, count to 10 slowly and take a deep breath.
- Always be polite, courteous, kind, respectful, and honest in dealings with students.

> **Integrity**
> If we work together, I know we can do this.
> *Never let the students catch you in a lie!*
>
> **Self-Control**
> Count to 10 and take a deep breath.
> Let me move out of this situation for a minute.
> I'll be right back.

ESTABLISHING LIMITS AND EXPECTATIONS

To have a positive learning environment, the teacher must establish limits and expectations. Children seek out structure and limits. Expec-

> It is important to establish and enforce the positive behaviors needed from the students that lead to the maximum academic success possible.

tations provide the students with guidelines for behavior. Limits without consequences are worthless. Consequences not enforced lead to loss of control by the teacher, allowing negative behaviors to eat away at the foundation of a positive learning environment.

Post classroom rules in a central location. Set classroom expectations high. This will provide a goal for the students to obtain. The basic classroom rules should be easy to reach. What do you want the students to do? When introducing new activities or assignments, reinforce the classroom limits by giving verbal reminders of wanted positive behaviors as well as unwanted negative behaviors. Are you clearly stating the specific behaviors you want of the students? Are the students aware of the classroom rules, your expectations, and the negative and positive consequences for behaviors?

The general Essential Character Discipline expectations for students are these:

1. Be polite to others.

2. Be faithful in the completion of academic activities.

3. Be considerate of others.

4. Do your best to complete all activities.

5. Give positive expressions of others.

6. Tell the truth.

7. Have self-control of words and actions.

The classroom teacher must verbally communicate the positive behaviors required for Essential Character Discipline and academic success, model the desired positive behaviors, and establish limits and expectations up front with students and parents. With the guidelines for behaviors established, presented, and explained, the students are provided with the structure needed to be successful in the academic setting.

To establish a successful learning environment, positive behaviors must be communicated verbally. The Essential Character Discipline Vocabulary, along with the rules, must be posted in the classroom and reviewed daily. The Essential Character Discipline Student Pledge/

Contract can be used to encourage self-respect, loyalty, perseverance, and self-control.

The Essential Character Discipline Student Pledge/Contract is as follows:

> I will practice the positive behavior of integrity.
>
> I will show honor for myself, my teachers, and my fellow students.
>
> I will be courteous when dealing with others.
>
> I will devote myself to the completion of my homework and assignments, while practicing perseverance when studying.
>
> I will respect myself and have self-control of my actions.

It is important to establish and enforce the positive behaviors needed from students that lead to the maximum academic success possible. To encourage the use of self- respect, loyalty, perseverance, and self-control, allow these basic classroom rules to be the foundation of your classroom rules:

1. Follow directions.
2. Complete assignments.
3. Work cooperatively with others.
4. Keep self and belongings in personal space.
5. Raise hand to speak in class.

SUMMARY

Essential Character Discipline is the necessary distinguishing feature of obedience to authority. Essential Character Discipline elicits order based on obedience to authority. Respect for self and others provides an environment of academic success established on self-control, perseverance, courtesy, loyalty, and respect.

The teacher is a powerful figure in the life of every student. To successfully manage the classroom in a positive manner that ensures academic success, the teacher must know a teacher's rights and know exactly the positive behaviors wanted from students. Children need the security of knowing the procedures, expectations, and limits of the academic setting. The Essential Character Discipline Vocabulary should be the foundation for the establishment of classroom rules (courtesy, loyalty, respect, perseverance, honor, integrity, and self-control).

In establishing classroom rules, the teacher should

1. Verbally communicate positive behaviors wanted
2. Model positive behaviors
3. Establish limits and expectations

It is important to establish and enforce the positive behaviors needed to lead to success in the classroom. Allow the basic classroom rules to be the foundation of classroom rules:

1. Follow directions.
2. Complete assignments.
3. Work cooperatively with others.
4. Keep self and belongings in personal space.
5. Raise hand to speak in class.

3

Let's Get Started

PLANNING FOR THE FIRST DAY
AND WEEK OF SCHOOL

Essential Character Discipline must begin the first day of school. To achieve your academic goals with your students, you need to plan how you will use the Essential Character Discipline Vocabulary daily to encourage the positive behaviors required to ensure academic success. The initial planning components to initiate the first day and week of school are these:

> On the first day of school, communicate the concept of Essential Character Discipline.

1. The positive behaviors (Essential Character Discipline Vocabulary) you want from the students

2. The posted copy of the Student Pledge/Contract

3. The positive consequences of academic success and self-esteem

On the first day of school, you must communicate the concept of Essential Character Discipline. Introduce the Student Pledge/Contract and distribute individual copies. Introduce the daily

> A positive working relationship with parents and guardians is essential in establishing behaviors needed to ensure academic success.

Rights of Parents

Parents have the right to

1. Ask for assistance from teachers and principals in developing Essential Character Discipline traits of their children

2. Feel secure in knowing their children's learning environment is a positive one that stresses academic success

Essential Character Discipline Vocabulary by defining the words and using them in sentences. Explain how the vocabulary, if incorporated into daily practice of all aspects of life, can lead to academic success.

The visual communication of Essential Character Discipline should include the following steps:

1. Make a chart of wanted positive behaviors.

2. Make a poster of the Student Pledge/ Contract.

3. Distribute copies of classroom positive behaviors.

4. Have students read and sign the Pledge/Contract stating the desire to model positive behaviors of Essential Character Discipline.

An example of opening day presentation of Essential Character Discipline by the classroom teacher is shown below.

Good morning, class. I am looking forward to a wonderful, positive, and successful academic school year. As your teacher, I will expect these seven essential behaviors from you: courtesy, loyalty, respect, perseverance, honor, integrity, and self-control. If we are all kind to one another, can depend on each other for help and assistance, appreciate each other for who we are, work hard and never quit, pay attention to each other, always tell the truth, and have self-control of our actions, then we will have a successful academic year. Every day, I expect you to

1. Follow directions.

2. Raise your hand to speak.

3. Keep yourself and your belongings in your personal space.

4. Complete assignments.

5. Always tell the truth.

Here is our Essential Character Discipline Pledge that will help us remember the positive behaviors that will govern our actions:

I will practice positive behaviors of integrity. I will show honor for myself, my teachers, and my fellow students. I will be courteous when dealing with others. I will devote myself to the completion of my homework and assignments, while practicing perseverance when studying. I will respect myself and have self-control of my actions.

I want you to take this copy of the pledge home to share with your family. Review this with your parents or guardians, get it signed, and return it tomorrow to me. Now let's copy the classroom rules on notebook paper. Please copy carefully and use your best handwriting.

Students who do not follow the rules will miss recess or assemblies or will be assigned detention after school. Students fighting will be referred to the office. We will follow the rules, respect self and others, and have control of our actions. We will all do our part to do what is right, so we can have a positive and successful school year. Do you have any questions?

At the end of the first week of school, send home a letter to parents and guardians restating the foundation of Essential Character Discipline. List the positive behaviors exhibited in the class during the week. This communicates to the parents and guardians that you are supportive and have established a positive academic learning environment. This initial communication establishes a positive, open relationship with the home. A positive working relationship with parents and guardians is essential in establishing behaviors needed to ensure academic success. An example of such a letter is shown in Resource F at the end of the book.

For any program to be successful, cooperation and positive interaction with the parents and guardians are required. The parent or guardian is the primary influence of the child's behavior and development. Positive interaction and modeling are essential in the development of just moral character. Academic success depends on the amount of support and assistance received from the parents and guardians. With teachers, parents, and the school working together and modeling the same positive behaviors, academic success is guaranteed.

For students to be successful, the parents or guardians have the responsibility to

1. Model positive behaviors and Essential Character Discipline

2. Assist the school with stressing the importance of positive behavior and academic success

ESSENTIAL CHARACTER DISCIPLINE AND THE PRINCIPAL

It is also necessary to establish a positive relationship with your principal. Once your discipline plan has been established for the school year, make copies of all essential materials and share them with your principal. Knowing that you have put forth an effort to establish defined objectives that lead to positive Essential Character Discipline will impress your principal. This meeting will allow you to discuss your plan and to know how much support you can expect from the principal.

Asking for Help From the Principal

When seeking assistance from the principal with negative, unwanted behavior from a student, it is logical to use the same method that you used with parents.

1. Keep the lines of communication open between you and the principal, so when assistance is needed with negative behaviors, you can ask for assistance without hesitation.

2. Have your goals and purpose written out before meeting with the principal. Know exactly what and how you would like the principal to assist you at that time.

3. Review Essential Character Discipline objectives with which the student is having trouble.

4. Verbally explain why you need assistance from the principal.

5. Be up-front with the principal about what you feel the consequences will be if you don't get support.

It is not guaranteed that you will get the parental/guardian involvement or the exact support you had hoped from the principal. You should have the satisfaction that you are doing your best to provide a positive learning environment that encourages academic success. With Essential Character Discipline in use in your classroom on a daily basis, you are providing your students with skills and behaviors that build character, self-esteem, and the thirst for knowledge.

BEHAVIOR PLAN

Essential Character Discipline should serve as the foundation of your positive behavior plan. Planning is of the utmost importance to good teaching. It takes careful step-by-step planning to successfully teach academic materials.

> Planning for productive academic success through positive behavior and discipline is a habit that needs to be as much of a teacher's routine as weekly lesson plans.

Academic lesson plans provide a structured guide to reach objectives. Modifications can be made in lesson plans to increase academic success. Planning for productive academic success through positive behavior and discipline is a habit that needs to be as much of a teacher's routine as weekly lesson plans.

What does Essential Character Discipline planning entail? It is the systematic application of the essential character principles presented in this book. It involves periodically, at the end of the day or week, evaluating the behavior of students to determine the positive behaviors exhibited by students, groups, and the class. For any school year to be successful, involvement of parents and guardians is a must. You have the right to ask for help from parents to ensure positive behaviors that lead to academic success.

COMMUNICATING WITH PARENTS AND GUARDIANS

> Be straightforward and up-front with the matter of consequences resulting from negative unwanted behaviors.

Clear, open communication with parents and guardians establishes the relationship needed to reinforce positive behaviors learned in school and at home.

1. Maintain weekly contact with parents to keep the positive lines of communication open.

2. When meeting with parents and guardians, have a goal or purpose.

3. Review Essential Character Discipline objectives.

4. Present rationale for meeting. Remind parents or guardians of their vital influence in the life and development of their child.

5. Explain the consequences if the parents or guardians are not cooperative in assisting in modeling the positive behaviors of Essential Character Discipline that lead to academic success.

6. Always have written documentation to support comments.

Maintain Contact

Many unwanted negative behaviors can be prevented if the parents and guardians are kept informed of the principles and philosophy of Essential Character Discipline. Notify parents or guardians that you will maintain weekly contact with them to develop a working relationship between the school and home. This will help establish and sustain parental involvement and support in the academic success of their child. This initial contact (a) sets the stage for hand-in-hand cooperation between the school and home, (b) keeps the lines of communication open and the parents and guardians informed of their child's progress, and (c) provides the parents and guardians with a sense of involvement that makes them feel at ease when contact with the school is necessary.

Establish Goals

Establish goals and purpose for meeting with parents and guardians. When it is necessary to meet with parents or guardians about negative or unwanted behaviors, know exactly what you want from the parent or guardian in the form of assistance and involvement. Have a copy of the Student Pledge, the Essential Character Discipline Vocabulary, and the philosophy of Essential Character Discipline.

Review Essential Character Discipline Objectives

Review the three rights of an educator that are needed to provide a positive academic learning environment (to encourage respect for self and others, to encourage self-control, and to ask for parental/guardian involvement). Review the three needs of the student that are required to provide a positive academic learning environment (respect and self-control; a teacher with respect for self and others; and help from parents and guardians, teachers, and principal).

Present Rationale for Meeting

Thank you for meeting with me today. It is in the best interest that we work together to develop and encourage positive behaviors here at school and in the community. Your involvement is most welcomed and encouraged. Your positive involvement and influence are of the utmost importance, if we are to encourage positive behavior. It is important that your child is aware that we are working together and that we will do all we can to encourage positive behaviors from your child.

Explain Consequences

Be straightforward and up-front with the parent or guardian on the matter of consequences resulting from unwanted behaviors. Provide the parent or guardian with a list of consequences resulting from negative behaviors (time-out, detention, removal from activities, denial of participation in group activities, and referral to the office). Inform the parent or guardian that the consequences for positive behaviors lead to positive self-esteem and academic excellence.

Provide Documentation

It is always wise to have complete written documentation to present to parents or guardians during a conference. Provide copies of assignments and records of positive and negative incidents to parents or guardians at this time.

When dealing with parents and guardians, use the principles of the Essential Character Discipline Vocabulary (courtesy, loyalty, respect, perseverance, honor, integrity, and self-control). When communicating with parents, (a) remain calm, (b) don't get defensive, (c) don't get angry, (d) review the philosophy of Essential Character Discipline, and (e) inform the parents or guardians that the child's academic success depends on the child's positive behaviors in the academic environment.

SUMMARY

Essential Character Discipline must begin the first day of school.

1. State the expected seven essential behaviors of courtesy, loyalty, respect, perseverance, honor, integrity, and self-control.

2. State daily expectations.

3. Review the Student Pledge/Contract.

4. Introduce the Essential Character Discipline Vocabulary.

5. Establish positive communication with parents and guardians. For any program to be successful, positive interaction and cooperation of the parents and guardians are required.

6. Establish a positive relationship with the principal. Provide the principal with a copy of your discipline plan.

7. Be prepared for meetings with parents and guardians.

Essential Character Discipline is a systematic program that models positive behaviors and academic success. Academic success lies in the amount of support and assistance received from parents and guardians. With the cooperation of teachers and parents or guardians in the modeling of the same positive behaviors, academic success is guaranteed.

4

Establishing Essential Character Discipline

How will Essential Character Discipline allow you to obtain positive responses from your students? As classroom teacher, you set the tone by providing the positive influence and model to assist the students in reducing negative behaviors. The teacher may be influential in a positive or a negative manner. When providing a learning environment of respect for self and others and perseverance in all efforts, the teacher establishes a supportive classroom.

Essential Character Discipline
1. Express expectations
2. Establish eye contact
3. Use nonthreatening gestures
4. Personalize messages
5. Provide warmth and support

COMMUNICATION

Express Expectations

The initial establishment of positive classroom behaviors is the manner in which Essential Character Discipline is communicated. Verbal communication is the first and foremost means of communicating your expectations. Verbally state the positive behavior wanted and the negative behaviors that are unwanted. Children, in general, welcome structure and like to know what is expected of them. There should be general rules and expectations that must be followed at all times, for example,

"You will have school supplies."
"You will get to school on time."
"There will be no fighting."
"You will use *thank you* and *please* in conversation."

How you verbally state your expectations are just as important as the expectations themselves. Your tone of voice and body language convey the message just as much as the content of the expectations. Eye contact, nonthreatening gestures, and use of students' names are helpful in ensuring that your expectations are communicated.

Establish Eye Contact

When conveying the expectations of Essential Character Discipline, always make eye contact with the students. Eye contact ensures that you have the students' attention. Eye contact also allows you to see if the message was received and understood.

Use Nonthreatening Gestures

Use nonthreatening gestures to gain the attention of students. It is important to remember to use gestures to give directions, get attention, and provide warmth and support. Never use threatening or hostile gestures that invoke fear, intimidation, or negative behaviors.

Personalize Message

When verbally stating expectations, use the name or names of students being addressed. Personalizing the message emphasizes the importance of your expectations and Essential Character Discipline. Using the student's name models the wanted positive behaviors of courtesy and respect for others. Personalizing the expectations ensures that the message will be received and comprehended.

Provide Warmth and Support

Physical contact in combination with a verbal message draws the child's attention to you and the message. A warm, supportive classroom is composed of expressions of concern, understanding, and kindness. Modeling this behavior illustrates to the students that it's okay to show positive outward expressions of warmth and concern.

In some situations, personal contact would not be appropriate. Some children do not like to be touched on the shoulder. With this knowledge, use other methods that can be just as effective. Always remember to model positive behaviors for all students.

When you explain the principles of Essential Character Discipline, its vocabulary, the Student Pledge, and the importance of positive behaviors in the academic setting,

1. Express your expectations and wanted behaviors in a matter-of-fact, direct tone of voice.

2. Establish eye contact with each student to ensure that your message is processed and understood.

3. Use nonthreatening gestures while walking around the room to obtain the attention of students and to establish a warm, supportive classroom setting.

4. Personalize your expectations by addressing students by name when providing examples of positive behaviors and inquiring about the understanding of your expectations.

5. Provide warmth and support with comforting taps on the shoulder while expressing expectations and explaining how exhibition of these positive behaviors can lead to academic success.

EXAMPLES

Providing daily examples of positive behaviors by the classroom teacher is vital to the success of Essential Character Discipline. The teacher must demonstrate verbal and visual models of the Essential Character Discipline Vocabulary.

1. Always provide polite remarks and gestures to your students and coworkers.

2. Always be loyal to your students by showing them through your actions that their welfare and education are of the utmost importance to you.

3. Always be willing to show consideration and concern for your students' feelings and their privacy.

4. Set the example of perseverance by always believing in your students and their ability to be successful in the classroom.

5. Honor your students by making them know and feel important to increase their self-esteem and morale.

6. Always be honest and up-front with your students about the importance of positive classroom behavior and academic success.

7. Maintain self-control in your actions and verbal expressions. A teacher who has self-control of personal actions has control of the classroom.

CONSEQUENCES

The backbone of the Essential Character Discipline management program is establishing and following through with consequences. To be influential in your academic learning environment, establish a list of five consequences that range from minor to severe for infractions of classroom rules and Essential Character Discipline (e.g., time-out, after-school detention, removal from activities or denial of participation in group field trips, call to parents, and referral to the office).

There must not be any excuse for the students' not knowing the positive behaviors expected of them, the unwanted negative behaviors, and the consequences for those negative behaviors.

When a student exhibits negative behaviors in the classroom, the teacher should take these steps:

1. State expectations of the student.

2. Explain how the unwanted behavior was not consistent with Essential Character Discipline principles.

3. Verbally state the consequences of the behavior.

4. Ensure that the student understands why the consequences are necessary.

With Essential Character Discipline, the students are responsible for their own actions. If they choose negative behaviors, they will have to accept the consequences without question. The classroom rules, Student Pledge/Contract, Essential Character Discipline Vocabulary, and consequences should be placed in a central, visible location for all to see. There must not be any excuse for the students' not knowing the positive behaviors expected of them, the unwanted negative behaviors, and the consequences for those negative behaviors.

To provide a learning environment of positive behaviors and academic success, consequences have to be established and carried out. Choose consequences that you will be able to enforce.

1. Consequences should never belittle or shame a child.

2. Consequences must never physically harm the student.

3. Consequences should be carried out as soon as possible.

4. When stating the consequences, remember to always model the Essential Character Discipline Vocabulary by exhibiting positive, nonthreatening behaviors and voice tone.

When it comes to follow-through with consequences, you as classroom teacher must show perseverance and avoid favoritism. Be persistent with your follow-through to show the students that you want to ensure that your classroom is one of positive behaviors that lead to academic success. For Essential Character Discipline to be successful, the students must realize that negative behaviors will not interfere in the educational process of your classroom.

Making and maintaining contact with the parents or guardians can help with consequences. The students need to know that from Day One, contact will be made with the parents or guardians and that both the home and school are working toward the same goals of positive classroom behavior and academic success through Essential Character Discipline. With parents and teachers working together to model positive behaviors and follow through with consequences for negative behaviors, the students learn to be responsible for their actions.

If you have explained the concepts of Essential Character Discipline and have made your class rules, Student Pledge/Contract, consequences, and Essential Character Discipline Vocabulary visible, the consequences must be carried out without hesitation when negative behaviors occur. Always keep accurate written documentation of negative and positive behaviors and consequences carried out to be prepared for conferences with parents or guardians and the principal.

SUMMARY

As the classroom teacher, you set the tone for behavior and academic performance. Essential Character Discipline establishes a supportive classroom. Express expectations, establish eye contact, use nonthreatening gestures, personalize messages of wanted behaviors, and provide warm support for your students. To be influential in the classroom, establish consequences and be consistent with follow-through of consequences. When negative behaviors are exhibited,

1. State your expectations.
2. Explain how the negative behavior was not consistent with Essential Character Discipline.
3. Verbally state the consequences.
4. Ensure that the student understands the reason for the consequences.

Consequences should never belittle, never cause physical harm, and never be delayed. Always model positive, nonthreatening behaviors and follow through with consequences for negative behaviors. This allows the students to learn responsibility for their own actions.

5

Negative Behaviors

Essential Character Discipline can be used to modify common negative behaviors of childhood. Students with anxious, impressionable, antagonistic, and self-centered behaviors can be motivated to develop positive behaviors in an environment conducive to academic learning and success. With a concerned educator who models the positive behaviors of courtesy, loyalty, respect, perseverance, honor, integrity, and self-control, negative behavior patterns can be modified, and students can be inspired to reach their fullest potential in behavioral management and academics.

ANXIOUS BEHAVIORS

Children who exhibit anxious behaviors are uneasy because of thoughts of fear about the possibility of coming misfortunes or trouble. These worries cause unsettled feelings or troubled thoughts. Anxious children have easily excited nerves and may be jumpy, restless, uneasy, or timid.

> There must not be any excuse for the students not knowing the positive behaviors expected of them, the unwanted negative behaviors, and the consequences for those negative behaviors.

Characteristics

Anxiety is one of many emotions that display a perplexing range of behaviors. Playing major roles in the development of anxiety are worry, stress, fear, lack of self-esteem, and/or the child's natural disposition. Fear and lack of self-confidence make anxious children their own worst enemy. They are tentative in approaching all life's daily requirements. Examples of anxious behaviors include the following:

+ Misinterpreting others
+ Being overly sensitive to constructive criticism
+ Exhibiting highly emotional outbursts
+ Not forgetting nonsense remarks
+ Not believing others
+ Having self-doubt and low self-esteem
+ Being preoccupied with minor concerns
+ Asking the same questions repeatedly
+ Wanting proof of actions
+ Feeling rejected when not given attention

Children who exhibit anxious behaviors are overly worried about the evaluation of self by others. Some anxious children do what is expected of them by peers to calm their own self-doubts. Approval in any form for any reason gives a brief moment of relief in efforts to please others. The decision-making process provides discomfort to children with anxious behaviors because they want to please others. They undergo great pressure when called on to make a decision that will not satisfy everyone.

Indecisive qualities give way to many negative behavioral characteristics:

+ Decreased value of responsibility
+ Seen as undependable
+ Disregard of creative methods to problems
+ Lack of sense of accomplishment
+ Skills not developed to potential
+ Fear of anything new
+ Pleasing no one, not even self

- Unclear communication skills
- Lack of self-esteem
- Ignoring own emotions
- Being taken advantage of by others

Children with anxious behaviors are in a losing situation because of pressure and sadness from trying to please everyone.

Physical Discomforts and Anxious Behaviors

Children with anxious behaviors commonly experience symptoms of physical discomforts. Physical discomforts that appear to have no medical basis are often signs of anxiety out of control. Listed below are some of the common physical discomforts associated with anxious behavior.

- Nervous stomach
- Tension headaches
- Fatigue
- Bed-wetting
- Sleep disturbances
- Low tolerance to minor injuries
- Low-grade fever
- Hyperventilation
- Dizziness
- Increased heart rate

Essential Character Discipline and Anxious Behaviors

Essential Character Discipline provides anxious children with daily guidance and examples to allow them to effectively confront their fears. Through respect, perseverance, and self-control, children with anxious behaviors are allowed to take charge of their out-of-control emotions. The positive environment of Essential Character Discipline provides guidance and support through anxious situations, while encouraging children to rely on their inner resources and strength to confront their fears. The systematic management program of Essential Character Discipline does not overprotect the children but helps them become more independent in making decisions and choices that will shape their lives. Children who are anxious need a greater degree of independence in their decision-making process.

The teacher communicates faith in the children's ability to respond to their fears. Listening is the most important communication tool of the teacher. Conveying to anxious children that they have been heard and understood allows them to face fears. Sometimes, verbal responses should be withheld until the children are less unsettled.

Essential Character Discipline provides a positive atmosphere that encourages relaxation as an alternative to anxiety. By displaying a relaxed nature, the teacher promotes a supportive classroom environment that offers the opportunity for relaxation. The teacher models a relaxed nature by

- ◆ Being determined when making decisions
- ◆ Not being prone to mood swings
- ◆ Being well organized
- ◆ Being hopeful and positive
- ◆ Having a good sense of humor
- ◆ Showing interest in the development of mind and well-being
- ◆ Being willing to admit to mistakes
- ◆ Being open to alternative views

The modeling of relaxed, nonanxious behaviors by the classroom teacher establishes an atmosphere of relaxation, independence, and perseverance for children with anxious behaviors.

Summary

Anxious behaviors include being

- ◆ Concerned
- ◆ Distressed
- ◆ Unsettled
- ◆ Disquieted
- ◆ Nervous
- ◆ Worried

Essential Character Discipline enables the classroom teacher to

- Be consistent with limits
- Communicate self-importance to children
- Model relaxation

IMPRESSIONABLE BEHAVIORS

Children who exhibit impressionable behaviors receive impressions readily from others. They are easily influenced by others, and their feelings are easily hurt or offended. Because they have an especially keen or delicate capacity for responding to external influences, such children are greatly affected by the feelings and emotions of peers and authority figures.

Characteristics

Impressionable behaviors are exhibited as a desire to obtain understanding from others. Children who are impressionable do not enjoy or invite friction. Their behaviors and wide range of emotions are a result of their emotional responses to others. They have sharp perceptions of what they think others think of them. Impressionable children are always noticing how others react to them. They are self-conscious and depend on the opinions of adults and peers. They are usually nonassertive around nonfamily members. Because of their deep emotional responses to others, their self-esteem is delicate. They downplay their sense of worth and importance. Impressionable children want communication that will promote understanding between themselves and others.

Barriers to Communication
With Impressionable Children

Offering a solution to a problem before children have given it enough thought is the main barrier to communication with impressionable children. Children with impressionable behavior first react to a problem with emotions, instead of rational thought. They feel that they must consider the total makeup of the problem. Negative behaviors may develop when the teacher provides the solution to the problem before the children understand their own emotions that resulted from the conflict.

Poor timing of honest communication and constructive criticism places impressionable children in the position of defending themselves. The teacher should not provide too much information or advice at first because this might cause impressionable children to rebel. Downsizing emotional reactions to disappointing events can leave the sensitive child feeling all alone with the problems. The teacher should avoid telling children not to act emotionally because the problem isn't serious or real—it's very serious and real to the children. They should be allowed to slowly work through the situation and their feelings about the situation.

Essential Character Discipline and Impressionable Behaviors

Essential Character Discipline provides children exhibiting impressionable behaviors with daily opportunities to develop a sense of self-worth, independence, coping skills, and communication skills. The classroom atmosphere is one that shows and provides respect for others' feelings and opinions. The teacher holds all students in high esteem and makes all students feel that they are important and necessary persons who contribute to the success of the class.

Children with impressionable behaviors should not be rescued from difficult circumstances. The teacher should not take responsibility for the behavior. Impressionable children need to learn the lesson of independence by taking the risks that lead to self-confidence.

Essential Character Discipline provides the daily guidelines that will help children who are impressionable develop responsible behavior. The classroom atmosphere encourages impressionable children to learn to function within the boundaries of their personal traits.

Essential Character Discipline provides a positive environment that is conducive to listening to children with impressionable behaviors. Listening provides the much needed emotional release for impressionable children. Compared with other children, impressionable children tend to be more honest in their communications. Essential Character Discipline provides an atmosphere of trust, which leads to open communication. Listening opens the door for the following:

- Decrease of severity of emotion
- Respect for the child's point of view
- Expressions of more feelings
- Establishment of rapport
- Reduction of guilt through sharing
- Acceptance, which encourages acceptance of self

Essential Character Discipline acknowledges the importance of individuality. Children who are impressionable need to know that they do not need to adapt to the guidelines of their vocal peer group. Essential Character Discipline does not try to change children's personalities but does provide an atmosphere that respects all and encourages positive behaviors and individual success.

Summary

Impressionable behaviors include being

- Sensitive
- Impressible
- Susceptible

Essential Character Discipline enables the classroom teacher to

- Allow children to learn natural control over their behavior
- Use good listening techniques
- Help students live within their limits

ANTAGONISTIC BEHAVIORS

Children who exhibit antagonistic behaviors are resistant and opposing. They fight, struggle, and contend against others. They are adversaries who actively oppose peers and authority. They can be hostile and easily make enemies. With unfavorable behaviors, they arouse dislike in others. In general, they obstinately oppose wanted behaviors that are reasonable or required. At times, children with antagonistic behaviors are stubborn and hard to control and have a fixed purpose or opinion.

They are unyielding, often unreasonable in doing things their own way, and, above all, determined to withstand any attempts to change their negative behaviors.

Characteristics

Children exhibiting antagonistic behaviors are in continual conflict with authority figures. They are ready to argue for no known reason. For antagonistic children, competition and aggression take the place of cooperation. Antagonistic children predictably

- Challenge authority
- Want to be in charge
- Cannot dispel emotional expressions of anger
- Favor competition to cooperation
- Demand quarrels
- Are insensitive to others

Antagonistic children want to place others in a power struggle. Frequent involvement in power struggles motivates behaviors of opposition. Antagonistic children never want to lose domination.

Essential Character Discipline and Antagonistic Behaviors

When teachers and other authority figures deal with antagonistic children, they must maintain control of their emotions so that antagonistic children do not use them to gain power and control. Limits and guidelines for behavior must be provided. The use of Essential Character Discipline places children with antagonistic behaviors in the position of maintaining responsibility for their own behavior. Consistency must be a part of the behavioral management program. If limits are not set and met, children will feel free to continue with oppositional behavior.

Communication and modeling of wanted behavior should include positive examples of the Essential Character Discipline Vocabulary. The teacher should avoid giving lectures to and arguing with antagonistic children. Unless otherwise requested to, the teacher should not provide opinions or advice but instead should learn to be a good listener. Children who are antagonistic need to be allowed to express their ideas and emotions to alleviate built-up pressure. Essential Character Discipline allows the teacher to develop rapport before a confrontation arises. Open communication lets children feel that they have voices and are heard. If children feel that they are listened to, they are more likely to cooperate. Respect for the children's feelings can be conveyed by nonverbal nudges, taps, hugs, and handshakes. Essential Character Discipline provides antagonistic children with the stability of knowing the procedures, expectations, and limits.

Summary

Antagonistic behaviors include being

◆ Oppositional
◆ Contrary
◆ Perverse

Essential Character Discipline enables the classroom teacher to

◆ Maintain control of emotions when dealing with antagonistic behaviors
◆ Establish boundaries and limits that allow children to be responsible for their behaviors
◆ Use perseverance in enforcing consequences for negative behaviors
◆ Provide an atmosphere that encourages open communication and understanding, making children more likely to choose positive behaviors

SELF-CENTERED BEHAVIORS

Children who exhibit self-centered behaviors are occupied with their own interest and affairs. They are overly concerned with themselves and are not concerned with the interest of peers or authority figures. In general, self-

> The atmosphere of the Essential Character Discipline classroom encourages children to come to the conclusion on their own that it is in their best interest to get along with others in a positive manner.

centered children are conceited, with too high opinions of their abilities or importance.

Characteristics

Self-centered children emphasize the importance of self. The outward expression of excess self-esteem is deceptive. These excessive outward expressions of self-centered children speak louder than actions in describing their true character.

Negative Self-Esteem	Positive Self-Esteem
Criticizes others	Encourages others
Holds grudges	Lets go of unnecessary anger
Will not accept criticism	Considers criticism
Makes demands	Knows limits
Uses deceptive communication	Uses open communication
Opinionated	Considerate of others
Withholds feelings	Open-minded
Preoccupied with self	Shares feelings
Moody	Has stable moods
Materialistic	Interested in others
Not satisfied with compliments	Emphasizes relationships
Enjoys others' failures	Enjoys others' success
Blames others for faults	Recognizes own limits

The behavior of children who are self-centered may be overly dramatized. When they experience loss of control, they feel a sense of panic. This fear leads to an explosion of behaviors when others do not respond to their need for control. This eruption is not an honest emotion but a trick of manipulation.

Relations with others are highly intense. Self-centered children work hard at building relationships. They want to be included and be known by a wide range of peers. Self-centered children are drawn toward those who will encourage and feel their need for control.

Irresponsible behavior is commonly displayed. Children with self-centered behaviors do not feel that the general rules and guidelines apply to them or that they should be held responsible for their actions.

The emotions of self-centered children are highly exaggerated. They have a strong feeling of elation when they experience success.

When they encounter disappointment, they become depressed. Any type of personal failure causes humiliation. Depression is a common emotion of self-centered children, although depression may be masked by indifference, outrage, or extreme display of pride.

Influencing Factors of Self-Centered Behaviors

The authority figure's good intentions may go amiss when the word *no* is not used at any necessary given time. Children who never hear the word *no* become thankless, ungrateful, and irresponsible. Too broad or too narrow boundaries also influence self-centered behaviors. Children, in general, do not respond well to too much constructive criticism or to adults who are too vague. Self-centered children have not been given appropriate behavioral boundaries. Lack of boundaries shades self-centered children from the needs of others. Children faced with too much or not enough direction from authority figures can develop self-centered behaviors.

Peer pressure encourages self-centered behavior. The influence of peer pressure is complex. Self-centered children do not realize how their own limitations can easily fall prey to the negative influences of peer pressure. Children who are self-centered are influenced by peer pressure because of the following:

- Desire to feel important
- Willingness to compromise values
- Willingness to assert self
- Fear of rejection
- Need for attention
- Willingness to allow popular vote to determine right and wrong

Essential Character Discipline and Self-Centered Behavior

The atmosphere of the Essential Character Discipline classroom encourages children to come to the conclusion on their own that it is in their best interest to get along with others in a positive manner. Essential Character Discipline establishes limits and consequences that are followed daily. Self-centered children are made aware that the class rules apply to all members of the class. The teacher maintains emotional control, models the examples of positive behaviors, and avoids communications that relay humiliation. Positive communication can encourage positive behaviors.

In the Essential Character Discipline classroom, the teacher avoids the following negative communications:

- Sarcasm
- Bringing up past negative events
- Threats that create confrontations
- Use of unfavorable colorful adjectives to describe personality
- Lectures without opportunities for children to respond
- Predictions of events resulting from poor choices
- Accusations that show lack of faith in the child

These negative behaviors are discouraged in an Essential Character Discipline classroom. Essential Character Discipline teaches behaviors that demonstrate and encourage responsibility. Some children have not been taught how to exhibit behaviors aimed at anything other than personal satisfaction. Essential Character Discipline teaches the importance of giving to others as part of the development of a well-rounded personality. Time must be allowed for self-centered children to determine that it is in their best interest to develop positive behaviors that require them to give of themselves to others. The Essential Character Discipline teacher provides a model of consideration for the needs of others beyond those that are self-centered and encourages positive social behaviors.

Summary

Self-centered behaviors include being

- Selfish
- Egotistical

Essential Character Discipline enables the classroom teacher to

- Provide an environment that allows students to see that positive behaviors are in their best interest

- ◆ Establish limits and consequences
- ◆ Maintain emotional control
- ◆ Avoid negative communication
- ◆ Provide a model of consideration

SUMMARY

To modify common negative behaviors of children, the teacher should model the positive behaviors of Essential Character Discipline. When dealing with antagonistic, impressionable, anxious, and self-centered behaviors, the concerned teacher models the positive behaviors of courtesy, loyalty, respect, perseverance, honor, integrity, and self-control to set examples that inspire all students to reach their fullest potential in behavioral management and academics. Essential Character Discipline enables the teacher to provide a positive atmosphere of relaxation to reduce anxious behaviors. The classroom atmosphere also encourages trust and open communication. Antagonistic behaviors are eliminated by the stability of the classroom environment, procedures, expectations, and limits. Students are well aware of established limits, consequences, and the applicability of class rules to all members of the class. Negative behaviors are not encouraged in an Essential Character Discipline classroom.

6

Emotional Behaviors

Essential Character Discipline can provide a supportive environment for children with depressed behaviors and dishonest behaviors. A major goal of childhood is for children to reach adulthood with a strong understanding of who they are as persons. On reaching adulthood, they will know their strengths and weaknesses and how to use them to live productive and happy lives. Depressed behaviors motivate children to feel insignificant compared with others and to grow into adults who do not recognize their value as persons. Because there are no established guidelines, too many children are given the message that deceitful behavior is okay. The lack of a sense of obligation to others encourages dishonesty. Environments that are lenient and without boundaries induce behaviors that do not recognize the need for honesty.

DEPRESSED BEHAVIORS

Children who exhibit depressed behaviors are gloomy, low-spirited, and full of sorrow. They are easily discouraged, and their self-esteem is low.

Characteristics

Depression is a long-lasting dissatisfaction with self and life in general. Children who are depressed have lost interest in normal daily activities. They are generally concerned with their own negative emotional state. Depressed children are also lethargic and may show signs of apathy such as the following:

- ◆ Remaining isolated
- ◆ Feeling unaccepted
- ◆ Frequently complaining
- ◆ Nonreaction to positive or negative events
- ◆ Undeveloped skills and abilities
- ◆ Unused developed skills
- ◆ Involvement in discovered negative behaviors
- ◆ Daydreaming frequently
- ◆ Failing to pursue relationships
- ◆ Not providing assistance
- ◆ Use of sarcasm
- ◆ Questioning the value of life
- ◆ Gloomy view of the future
- ◆ Considering rules useless

These apathetic behaviors express the depressed children's feelings of internal pressure. They use apathy to build a wall of protection to guard against emotional hurt that leads to future depression. Children who are depressed show a lack of competence and irresponsibility in a wide range of life activities, and their level of potential competence is not reached. Lack of academic success, poor family relations, or insufficient social confidence can lead to depression. Lack of personal value may be verbalized as follows:

"They will never miss me."
"She did not want my help anyway."
"He cannot really love me."
"They expect too much from me."
"I will never get it right."
"Why do I always lose?"
"What difference will it make if I know that?"
"I never get anything good. So why should I share?"
"They try to make my life miserable."

Children who are depressed do not understand their personal worth. They cannot reach out to others and do not use their skills to relate with others. Because they do not think that they are important, they have no direction in their lives.

Depressed children are cumbrous in the expression of their emotions. Despair is developed from the inability to communicate emotions. They think that ignoring a problem will make it disappear.

Risk-taking behavior increases with depression. Depressed children would rather risk bodily harm, social harm, or brushes with the law than face the loud emotional pains of depression.

Factors Influencing Depressed Behavior

Stress reactions may cause depression. The ever present negative patterns of depression exhaust children's self-worth. All children need to feel as if they belong. Incidents that cause stress can be traumatic. Stress factors include

- Failing grades
- Being overlooked
- Poor performance in sports
- Lack of friends
- Punishment or reprimand
- Arguments with family or friends
- Losing a pet
- Being turned down
- Onset of puberty
- Moving

Depressed feelings can be reinforced in a number of ways:

- Frequent advisory criticism
- Lack of one-on-one attention from authority figures
- Emotional communication tones
- Having accomplishments and achievements ignored
- Attention primarily for bad things
- Inconsistent follow-through on promises

Depressed children need structure and a supportive environment that provides positive attention and respect for their unique qualities.

Essential Character Discipline and Depressed Behaviors

Through Essential Character Discipline, the classroom teacher can help depressed children by

- Allowing them to have a voice in situations that are personally related to them
- Allowing respect for their opinions
- Providing a sincere role model
- Establishing nonchaotic schedules
- Giving praise for their individual qualities
- Giving healthy expressions of concern
- Providing a flexible atmosphere for individual needs
- Demonstrating a good sense of humor
- Establishing self-control in times of distress

Trauma and Depressed Behaviors

Traumas of life such as death, divorce, and physical harm lead to certain depression in children. When interacting with children dealing with life traumas, the teacher should use the principles of respect, integrity, loyalty, and honor.

Show honor by

- Never ignoring the reality of the trauma on children
- Refraining from trying to overprotect children after the trauma because children miss out on the opportunity of learning responsibility
- Trying not to give unnecessary details

Show integrity by

- Not hiding information when children are likely to be aware of the information

◆ Keeping the positive lines of communication open
◆ Providing children with undivided personal attention

Show loyalty by

◆ Keeping children out of controversial situations

Show honor by

◆ Allowing children to express opinions—negative and positive
◆ Being patient when children are in a state of transition
◆ Allowing children to talk about the trauma whenever and as long as needed

Positive Comments

Make positive comments count. Children who are depressed need and want to know that they are held in high esteem and are respected, especially if they have a low self-image. The teacher's comments must be positive, factual, and true. By encouraging a positive self-image, the teacher allows children to release themselves of emotional burdens that encourage depression.

Be spontaneous in providing rewards. Give unannounced rewards to motivate children with low self-esteem. Spontaneous rewards have a strong effect and cause the children to want to repeat the behaviors that provide the pleasant surprise.

Communication

Allow the children to talk freely. The environment of Essential Character Discipline classrooms encourages the teacher to be available so the children can speak freely. The principles of Essential Character Discipline foster the understanding of the children's views.

Nonverbal expressions and body language should indicate sincere interest in the children. Silence allows them to gather and organize their thoughts. When communicating with depressed children, ask questions to gather information, rather than place blame or imply guilt or wrongdoing. If the teacher maintains control of her or his emotions, then the children maintain a state of calmness.

Disagreements are to be expected. Show respect for the children by the use of positive vocal tones, open posture, and nonthreatening gestures. Depressed children gain a better understanding of themselves by their interactions with adults in authority. The teacher who listens can bring about positive changes in the depressed children's behavior.

The Essential Character Discipline
Teacher and Depressed Behaviors

The teacher provides guidance and positive behavioral examples. These positive traits are

- Emotional stability
- Self-concept not dependent on material gain
- Sincerity
- Living within rules
- Communicating values
- Listening to and valuing others' opinions
- Respect for others
- Encouraging cooperation
- Providing for others' needs
- Keeping promises

Summary

Depressed behaviors include being

- Dejected
- Heavyhearted
- Dispirited

Essential Character Discipline enables the classroom teacher to

- Provide an environment free from lingering feelings of tension
- Provide an environment of unity and support
- Make positive verbal comments
- Provide spontaneous rewards

- Model positive behavioral traits
- Be a good listener
- Let children speak freely

DISHONEST BEHAVIORS

The prime objective of children who exhibit dishonesty is to make others believe something true is false. Dishonest behaviors consist of deceiving, lying, and/or cheating. Children practice dishonest tricks either verbally or by false, misleading representation. They may twist the truth to mislead and gain advantage over others. They are always ready and willing to deceive.

> Essential Character Discipline is a daily classroom management program that continually develops stronger self-images, instead of being implemented after children have engaged in negative behaviors.

Characteristics

Several negative behaviors are common in the characteristic of deceitfulness. Many children who exhibit dishonest behaviors do not admit to their feelings of inferiority or their need for recognition. These children generally want to please others although they are aggressive toward peers and argumentative with adults. Their well-established pattern of misconduct is an apparent lack of integrity.

Lying, cheating, and stealing have different meanings for children at varied age levels. Preschoolers may steal and lie about it because they saw something they wanted and took it. Teens may steal and lie about it to obtain the recognition and acceptance of peers for being daring and bold. The risk of being detected in the act increases the thrill of the negative behavior.

Manipulation hides the deeper feeling of insecurity of children who are dishonest. They may use manipulation to hide the emotion of anger or as a way of expressing dissatisfaction. Dishonest children use manipulation to avoid receiving attention. Some children use manipulative tactics to experience the feelings of power or control. Deceit is generally used to cover the deeper feelings of personal inferiority. Irresponsibility is a common characteristic of dishonest children. They are

quick to recognize opportunities to take the easy way out of an
assigned task and usually take advantage of these opportunities.
   General practices of irresponsible behaviors include

 ◆ Failure to accept challenges within range of ability
 ◆ Taking shortcuts instead of completing task
 ◆ Using illness or injury as an excuse
 ◆ Using confusing explanations
 ◆ Accusing others of messing things up
 ◆ Not completing assignments
 ◆ Creating diversions to take emphasis off task
 ◆ Chronic forgetfulness
 ◆ Persistent procrastination
 ◆ Inability to work without direct supervision
 ◆ Coaxing others to do their work for them
 ◆ Claiming ignorance
 ◆ Allowing deadlines to pass to make it impossible to complete
    task
 ◆ Complaining that "no one else has to do it"
 ◆ Claiming unfair treatment by others

   Children who exhibit dishonest behaviors are quick to point the fin-
ger of blame toward other people or situations. Any other behavior
would expose the dishonest children's involvement in counterfeit
behavior.

Communication

   The communication of dishonest children with others is somewhat
unclear. Expressions of emotions and feelings can be communicated
verbally or nonverbally. Some emotions are communicated openly,
whereas others are transmitted by implications of words or actions.
Other emotions are expressed through behavior patterns. Nonverbal
communication will give strong clues to the children's feelings. Without careful observation of the children's behavior, they will experience
repeated success in sending distorted, inaccurate messages to others.

This successful distortion prevents children with dishonest behaviors from owning up to the reality that they fear.

Dishonesty may encourage children to forcefully deny their emotions with strong verbal responses. Deceitful behaviors create a serious communication problem for children. If children communicate their feelings honestly, they then draw attention to past efforts to cover up the same or similar feelings. To prevent exposure as frauds, dishonest children continue to cover up true feelings and emotions. The dishonest children's expressed behaviors and inner feelings do not match because they do not want to be revealed as phonies. They disguise their internal beliefs in many ways:

- ◆ Playing the role of an expert or a know-it-all
- ◆ Intellectualizing a problem to avoid discussing the emotions involved
- ◆ Laughing inappropriately at others
- ◆ Giving in to peer pressure despite signs of potential harm
- ◆ Refusing to state a belief
- ◆ Overstating a belief
- ◆ Associating only with those in the elite "in" crowd
- ◆ Pretending to be interested when there is no interest
- ◆ Working too hard to make a positive impression

Children who are dishonest assume that others are being fooled by their behavior. They are confident that no one will discover the discrepancy between their inner feelings and their outward behavior. Although dishonest children fear that their deception will be detected, they still continue the same deceitful behavior.

The pride of dishonest children reaches an unhealthy level. Pride allows children to develop a positive respect for themselves, but children who are dishonest allow pride to exaggerate the sense of importance placed on themselves. Pride affects dishonest children in many ways:

- ◆ An increased importance is placed on reputation among peers.
- ◆ Arrogance is used to mask shortcomings.
- ◆ The reactions of others are received with a high level of sensitivity.

- ◆ True feelings and emotions are not expressed.
- ◆ Constructive criticism causes anger instead of change.
- ◆ Personal weaknesses are not correctly recognized.
- ◆ When others take a leadership position, discomfort arises.

Excess pride encourages children to exhibit behaviors that communicate all is well, when in fact they are miserable.

Factors Influencing Dishonest Behaviors

Fear of Others' Reactions

Dishonest children lie because they don't like the consequences of admitting their wrongdoing. Children do not want to be punished, scolded, criticized, or embarrassed. Deceitful behavior is followed up by attempts to avoid being caught in the act and being held accountable for actions. The fear of negative responses from peers or authority figures motivates children to continue in negative, self-defeating patterns of behavior.

Attention From Others

All children are in need of reassurance from others that they are important. Positive attention provides children with the most common security of value and self-worth. Seeking attention from others, dishonest children go too far with negative behaviors to obtain this attention.

Pressure to Succeed

Pressure from others to meet given standards prompts some children to exhibit negative behaviors to relieve stress and emotional strain. They become deceitful to escape their troubles. Pressure to succeed exists for all children.

Pressures facing teens include

- ◆ Expectations of significant adults
- ◆ Friends
- ◆ School
- ◆ Sports
- ◆ Wanting to be independent

- Fear of being forced to be independent
- Resentment toward authority
- Fitting in with peers
- Continuous introduction to new situations
- Jealousy of siblings
- Confronting fears of being alone, the dark, public speaking
- Need for assurance

Pressures of adolescence include

- Peer expectations
- Temptation to experiment with alcohol, drugs, and sex
- Being in a prestigious group
- Identity crises
- Criticism from authority figures
- Financial independence
- Interaction with opposite sex
- Increased awareness of social issues
- Desire to accumulate material items
- Making important choices about future

Essential Character Discipline and Dishonest Behaviors

There are two areas to focus on when dealing with dishonest children.

1. Look at the deceitful behavior itself. Reinforcement must be given to discourage dishonesty and encourage truthfulness. Essential Character Discipline provides an environment that models positive behaviors, limits, and consequences.

2. Look for reasons for the deceitful behavior. Not understanding the reason for the negative behavior encourages a repeat of the maladjusted behavior. Essential Character Discipline encourages positive, open communication between the classroom teacher and students. Open lines of communication encourage the students to freely and honestly talk about feelings and behaviors.

The Essential Character Discipline teacher does not react emotionally to children's expression of their thoughts and feelings. The major objective of Essential Character Discipline is for children with dishonest behavior to conclude for themselves the way they should handle their problems. Children who are able to freely communicate their thoughts, feelings, and emotions are more likely to develop positive patterns of honest communication that is free of deceit.

Avoid emotional reactions that will hurt the children. Confrontation is a common reaction to dishonesty. Keep in mind that an angry outburst produces negative feelings in the children, and these negative emotions produce a bitter war of words.

Dishonest children recognize a threat as a challenge, thrill, and/or excitement. A threat will be challenged just to see if more problems can be created. Firm guidelines, not threats, should be established.

One way to break down communication with children is to publicize or broadcast their negative behavior. The children will be extremely hurt and humiliated.

Do not ask "why" questions. Claiming ignorance allows children to continue the deceitful pattern of negative communication. Avoid "why" questions because an honest answer is not likely to be provided.

The positive response to children exhibiting dishonest behavior is a brief statement of honest emotions that provides behavioral limits and consequences, followed by a normal pattern of communication as soon as possible. The silent treatment only draws out the problem and encourages new opportunities for dishonest exchanges.

Take action based on the available information. Dishonest children may use confusion as a tactic. They want to keep the adult guessing about what really happened. They also want to make sure the adult is uncertain about the children's role in the negative behavior. When children are in control, negative behaviors that develop are not in their best interest. Assume control, and act on the best information available.

The consequences should match the behavior. Essential Character Discipline holds the children responsible for deceitful behavior but provides a model and positive behaviors that will increase the likelihood that other similar negative behaviors will not reoccur. Children are deceitful because of fear of what might happen if the truth were known. They will continue to be deceitful if being honest results in severe punishment.

Deceitfulness is an awkward attempt to let others know that something inside feels wrong. The communication of emotions through deceitful behaviors draws attention to the misbehavior and away from the underlying emotional need. Essential Character Discipline is a daily classroom management program that continually develops stronger self-images, instead of being implemented after children have engaged in negative behaviors.

Essential Character Discipline provides an environment that shows positive feelings to children exhibiting dishonesty. The Essential Character Discipline classroom provides daily positive models to strengthen dishonest children's self-image.

- Say the child is important.
- Spend individual time with each child.
- Provide hugs and friendly gestures.
- Say "I admire you" regularly.
- Provide nonverbal messages through pleasant facial expressions.
- Verbally recognize worth of children in front of others.
- Tell children that they are competent.
- Provide specific information about the value of a task well done.
- Congratulate children for correcting mistakes.
- Chart the children's progress and give positive comments.
- Assign tasks that children can complete successfully.
- Ask children to describe an event or serve as peer tutors.

Summary

Dishonest behavior is being

- Deceitful
- Misleading

Essential Character Discipline enables the classroom teacher to

- Look at the dishonest behavior
- Model positive behavior
- Look for reasons for the dishonest behavior

- Keep lines of communication open between student and teacher
- Establish firm guidelines, not threats
- Not publicize negative behaviors
- Respond with brief honest emotions and behavioral limits and consequences
- Develop children's positive self-image

The primary goal of Essential Character Discipline is to present students with positive behaviors. The principles of Essential Character Discipline set the stage for daily exposure to positive modeling of wanted behaviors, open communication, and academic achievement. Children seek structure and guidelines. Essential Character Discipline provides a structured environment, positive role models, and opportunities for academic success for all children.

SUMMARY

Essential Character Discipline provides an environment that works on developing a stronger self-image. The overall aim of Essential Character Discipline is to provide an environment conducive to academic success, developing self-esteem and positive self-concepts, and developing the student's respect for self and others. The concerned teacher models the positive behaviors of courtesy, loyalty, respect, perseverance, honor, integrity, and self-control to set examples that inspire all students to reach their fullest potential in behavioral management and academics.

7

Consequences for Positive Behaviors

VERBAL PRAISE

What is your general response to students who exhibit positive behaviors? Positive behaviors should always be rewarded with positive verbal responses. The basic principle of Essential Character Discipline is to model desirable behav-

> Positive behaviors should always be rewarded with positive verbal responses.

iors of respect, courtesy, and integrity. Always remember to respond favorably to students who are contributing to the supportive nature of the learning environment. Verbal praise for wanted behavior places you in the position to motivate your students to increase desired behaviors and academic achievement.

All students seek structure and recognition. Responding to positive behaviors will motivate students to continue with those behaviors. Showing your students that you are truly interested in their conduct and academic success will reduce the time needed for addressing negative behaviors. Essential Character Discipline provides the students with information needed to choose behaviors that will lead to a favorable classroom environment and academic attainment.

Positive behaviors create a positive classroom environment. Learning cannot take place in an environment that is dominated by negative behaviors. The main objective of Essential Character Discipline is to assist you in developing and modeling behaviors that will lead to academic success and learning. The more you encourage positive behaviors through verbal praise, the better the children will feel about themselves, their classroom, and the importance of academic achievement. It is important that you know the positive behaviors wanted from your students.

For your verbal responses to be effective, they should be

1. Positive words of encouragement that show concern, appreciation, and respect
2. Provided as soon as possible after a positive behavior has been observed

Select sincere verbal responses that you feel comfortable using. The delivery of your response is important. Listed below are suggestions of positive verbal reinforcement to provide to students. Be sure to let the parents know about the praise you give their children.

You're the best	Great	You tried harder
Keep up the good work	You go the extra mile	Terrific
Dedicated to excellence	Your love shines through	Thanks for
We love you	Every day you make	helping
Outstanding	us better	You're number
You made our day	You're sensational	one
You're a success	Hooray for you	Good job
You're wonderful	That's incredible	Beautiful work
Way to go	Bravo	Fantastic effort
We appreciate you today	Fantastic	Right on target
Excellent	We're proud of you	You're important
Wonderful	You're a winner	Superstar
Remarkable job	Well done	You deserve
Phenomenal	Awesome	a hug
Cream of the crop	World class	You're
We respect you	You're a trooper	spectacular
Your heart is in	You're a born leader	Magnificent job
the right place	We knew you could	You're unique
You're amazing	do it	Team player
You make our day	You are very	We love you
Remarkable talent	responsible	Incredible

Shining dedication	Thank you	Super
100% dedication	You're perfect	Dynamite
Outstanding effort	You're a true friend	You're a joy
One of a kind	Fabulous	I'm happy
VIP	A hidden treasure	Beautiful
The BEST	Great going	

Essential Character Discipline does not encourage the use of tangible consequences for wanted positive behaviors. The students need to realize that some behaviors are carried out because they are right and contribute to academic success. Surprises, special events, and tangible rewards should be incorporated into the daily plan of your Essential Character Discipline program for all students as a group to provide an environment of respect, integrity, and academic excellence.

POSITIVE CONTACT WITH PARENTS

Positive notes and phone calls to students' homes greatly reinforce desired classroom behaviors. Keeping the parents or guardians informed lets them know that you appreciate and support positive classroom behavior.

Continuing contact between home and school is an advantage. When parents are involved in a positive manner with the school, students are more successful academically and emotionally, and home and school performances are enhanced. Attendance, grade point averages, and classroom behaviors improve with close communication between the school and home. The lack of a positive relationship between school and home leads to negative behaviors.

Teachers should be aware of negative behaviors that create barriers to positive home-school relationships. Adverse factors that may undermine relationships between teachers and parents include the following:

1. Attitudes of parents
   - Some parents feel that they have to compete with the teacher.
   - Some parents blame the school for the child's negative behavior.

- Some parents feel inferior, helpless, or powerless when dealing with the school.

2. Attitudes of teachers
   - Some teachers feel that they have to compete with the parents.
   - Some teachers blame the parents for the child's negative behavior.
   - Some teachers feel threatened by parents because of lack of confidence in their own ability.

3. Logistical concerns
   - Communication time between parents and teachers is too limited.
   - The typical home-school conference is not an effective problem-solving session.
   - The typical home-school relationship is not a purposeful one.
   - It is difficult for parents to arrange transportation and time off from work to establish positive home-school relationships.

4. Skills in communication
   - In some cases, neither the parent nor the teacher has effective communication skills to maintain positive home-school relationships.

5. Philosophical concerns
   - Some parents believe that the academic decision-making process is the responsibility of the teacher.

What can you as the teacher do to foster positive home-school relationships? There is no one type of home-school relationship, but all relationships should be positive. Some parents choose to be passive participants, whereas others want to be active in the decision-making process. Keep relationships with parents flexible, open, and affirmative. Here are some things you can do to improve relationships with parents:

1. Write personal notes.
2. Send weekly progress reports.
3. Make "good news" phone calls.
4. Prepare parents for conferences by sending information to be discussed.

AWARDS

The teacher may design special awards for positive classroom behaviors and academic achievement. These awards may be weekly and/or monthly. Students who model wanted positive behaviors need encouragement and reinforcement. Buttons, certificates, or ribbons can be great motivators. Sample award certificates are shown in Resource G.

CONTRACTS

At the beginning of the school year, each student is asked to read and sign the Essential Character Discipline Pledge/Contract (Resource E). After reading the pledge, the teacher reviews the definitions and meanings of the seven words of Essential Character Discipline Vocabulary and gives examples of positive behaviors wanted in the classroom. Listed below are some examples of wanted positive behaviors.

Courtesy: Saying thank you, please, you're welcome, excuse me, yes, no

Loyalty: Attending class daily, completing assignments, keeping classroom clean

Respect: Taking turns, sharing, listening to others, using quiet voices

Perseverance: Daily studying, staying on task

Honor: Paying attention, following directions, raising hands to speak

Integrity: Following school and class rules, telling the truth

Self-Control: No fighting or using profanity, no stealing, no cheating

The contract is an agreement between the teacher and the student. Issuing the contract on the first day of school lets the students know what is expected of them. The contract ties in with the rights of the teacher, the students, and the parents or guardians. Sending the contract home to be signed by the parents informs them of the positive behaviors that the students will try to accomplish during the school year.

Traditional rewards for individual positive behaviors will not be necessary with the use of Essential Character Discipline because of the practical modeling of positive behaviors by the teacher. Parties or treats should be used not as rewards for behaviors but as opportunities for the entire class to practice the principles of Essential Character Discipline.

SUMMARY

Positive behaviors should always be rewarded with verbal praise. Positive responses to positive behaviors will motivate students to continue the desired conduct. Essential Character Discipline provides an environment of respect, integrity, and academic excellence that encourages positive classroom behaviors.

Establishing regular contact with the parents and reinforcing positive relationships between the school and home can lead to and encourage the elimination of negative classroom behaviors. Be aware of the negative behaviors that can create barriers to positive home-school relationships in the areas of attitudes of parents, attitudes of teachers, logistical concerns, communication skills, and philosophical concerns.

Improve relationships with the home by

1. Writing personal notes

2. Sending weekly progress reports

3. Making "good news" phone calls

4. Sending conference information in advance to parents

Conclusion

The foundation of Essential Character Discipline is the positive modeling influence a teacher can have on the behavior of students. Providing a classroom that fosters courteous conduct, obedience, self-esteem, determination, self-respect, honesty, and self-control will lead to academic success. The responsibility of the teacher is to provide knowledge and understanding of the Essential Character Discipline Vocabulary that encourages students to exhibit positive behaviors and strive for academic excellence.

The primary goal of Essential Character Discipline is to expose students to positive behaviors. With the introduction of the Essential Character Discipline Vocabulary on a daily basis across the board, the learning environment becomes one that encourages respect for self, others, and academic achievement. Essential Character Discipline promotes positive communication between the school and the parents. The relationship between positive classroom behaviors and academic success must be established and understood by the parents for the students to be successful in their academic careers. Essential Character Discipline pro-

> There is a war going on in our American society. We hear about it every day. The battle is between positive and negative behaviors. There are many casualties and prisoners of war, and a large majority of both are our children. To put a stop to the negative behaviors and destruction, we must establish Essential Character Discipline in the daily routine of our children.

vides the classroom teacher with the tools needed to establish a positive environment. A positive classroom setting leads to productivity, comprehension, and academic success. With increased positive behaviors, self-esteem, and respect for self and others, the students are inspired to reach their highest potentials. The modeling of courtesy, loyalty, respect, perseverance, honor, integrity, and self-control by the classroom teacher sets the tone for positive behaviors and academic achievement in the classroom.

> The purpose of Essential Character Discipline is not to "catch kids being good" but to establish and develop the positive behaviors required to build the character and self-esteem that kids need to do the right thing and be responsible for their own actions and behaviors.

There is a war going on in our American society. We hear about it every day. The battle is between positive and negative behaviors. There are many casualties and prisoners of war, and a large majority of both are our children. To put a stop to the negative behaviors and destruction, we must establish the principles of Essential Character Discipline in the daily routine of our children: courtesy, loyalty, respect, perseverance, honor, integrity, and self-control. If these positive behaviors and their importance to academic success are taught, society as a whole will improve. Today, too many children are growing up without respect for self and others. Essential Character Discipline incorporates self-respect, perseverance, and self-control into the academic setting, which encourages positive behaviors that lead to academic achievement and self-esteem.

Using Essential Character Discipline in the classroom will rebuild the moral fiber and character of this country and encourage academic success at all levels. The purpose of Essential Character Discipline is not to "catch kids being good" but to establish and develop the positive behaviors required to build the character and self-esteem that kids need to do the right thing and be responsible for their own actions and behaviors.

Resource A

Glossary

Adherence: Devotion and support to a cause.

Admiration: The sense of wonder and delight of a person, place, or thing.

Admire: To regard with wonder, delight, and approval.

Adoration: Great love and respect for a person.

Allegiance: Loyalty or devotion to a person or cause.

Appreciation: Grateful recognition.

Assurance: Belief in one's own abilities.

Attention: Thoughtful consideration for others.

Balance: Ability to make decisions.

Behavior: The way a person acts.

Bold: Confident.

Bond: A duty or promise.

Brave: Willing to face danger, pain, or trouble without being afraid.

Certainty: Acting without a doubt.

Character: A statement about a person's behavior.

Charity: An act of goodwill or kindness.

Citizenship: A person's behavior as a citizen.

Compassion: Feeling of sorrow for the suffering of others.

Conduct: The way a person acts or behaves.

Conscience: Knowing the difference between right and wrong.

Conscientious: Behaving according to what one knows is right.

Consideration: Careful thought or attention.

Constancy: State of not changing; staying the same.

Continue: To endure or go on.

Conviction: Strong belief in something.

Cordiality: Warm friendly feelings or actions.

Courage: Bravery; quality of being without fear.

Courtesy: A polite, helpful, or considerate act or remark.

Credit: Acknowledgment of work completed.

Decision: Act of making up one's mind.

Deference: Courteous regard or respect.

Dependable: Reliable or trustworthy.

Determination: Quality of never giving up.

Devoted: Dedicated to a person or cause.

Dignity: Being worthy of honor.

Duty: Obedience or respect that one shows to parents.

Elevation: A high place or position.

Endure: To hold up and last under pain and stress.

Energy: Strength or power expressed.

Essential: Absolutely necessary.

Esteem: To appreciate someone greatly.

Faith: Complete trust in someone or something.

Faithful: Showing a strong sense of responsibility.

Fearless: Not afraid.

Fidelity: Faithful devotion to a person or cause.

Fixate: To be steady and not moving.

Fortitude: Ability to bear misfortune calmly.

Friendly: Kindly, supportive, and helpful.

Gallantry: Heroic courage.

Generosity: Willingness to share with others.

Good: Well-behaved.

Good-natured: Agreeable.

Good-tempered: Not easily angered.

Goodness: Quality of being well behaved.

Gracious: Showing kindness.

Grit: Always being brave.

Heart: Feelings of love, devotion, sympathy, or enthusiasm.

Heed: To pay close attention to someone or something.

Honest-to-goodness: Real.

Honesty: Absence of lying, cheating, or stealing.

Honor: Something done or given for good behavior.

Independence: Freedom from the control of others.

Integrity: Honesty and sincerity.

Intestinal fortitude: Courage.

Justice: Fairness to self and others.

Kindness: The habit of being considerate.

Loyal: Supportive of a person or cause.

Loyalty: Faithfulness to an idea or person.

Manner: The way one acts.

Moral: Knowing the difference between right and wrong.

Note: To observe certain characteristics or features.

Notice: To observe and pay attention.

Obedience: Willingness to follow the rules.

Open: Not closed to new ideas.

Perseverance: Act of continuing with a task until it is completed.

Persist: To refuse to give up.

Poise: Calmness.

Polite: Showing good manners.

Popular: Appealing to the general public.

Praise: To express approval.

Pursue: To follow a particular plan.

Recognize: To acknowledge; to show appreciation

Refinement: Act of making improvements.

Regard: To show concern for a person.

Regulation: Rule.

Reliable: Dependable.

Remain: To stay while others go.

Renown: Great fame.

Reputation: How a person is seen by others.

Reserve: Keeping one's thoughts to self.

Resolution: Solving a puzzle.

Respect: To feel or show honor.

Respectability: Behaviors that show honor.

Responsibility: Something that others depend on you to do.

Restrain: To keep under control.

Restraint: Control of emotions.

Reverence: Feelings of deep love and respect.

Right: Following the law or rules.

Righteous: Doing what is right.

Safe conduct: Careful behavior.

Self-assurance: Confidence in one's ability.

Self-confidence: Belief in one's abilities.

Self-control: Regulation of one's emotions and actions.

Self-determination: Making decisions without influence from others.

Self-esteem: Pride and belief in self.

Self-government: Responsibility of a group for own actions.

Self-regard: Concern for one's own interest.

Self-reliance: Dependence on one's own judgment.

Self-respect: Showing honor for oneself as a person.

Self-restraint: Control of oneself.

Self-will: Carrying out one's own wishes.

Sincerity: Honesty.

Spunk: Courage.

Stability: Staying with a purpose.

Stamina: Ability to keep going even when tired.

Strength: Being strong.

Sympathy: Ability to have the same feelings as another person.

Tact: Knowing the right thing to say and do.

Tenacious: Strong and tough.

Thoughtful: Thinking in a careful manner.

Tribute: Something given to show honor and praise.

Trustworthy: Dependable and honest.

Truth: Honest facts.

Truthful: Stating facts.

Value: Importance.

Vigor: Active physical strength.

Virtue: Courage to be good.

Will: The particular choice of a person.

Word of honor: Verbal promise.

Resource B

Vocabulary Activities

INTRODUCTORY ACTIVITIES

◆ Introduce daily Essential Character Discipline Vocabulary.
◆ Orally and visually present definitions of vocabulary words.
◆ Use the vocabulary words in written sentences.
◆ Give and ask for examples of actions and behaviors that demonstrate the vocabulary word for the day.

LANGUAGE EXPRESSION ACTIVITIES

◆ Journal entries: Have students use daily vocabulary word in their journals.
◆ Have students write the definition of the daily vocabulary word.
◆ Have students write three sentences telling why it is important to exhibit the actions of the vocabulary word.
◆ Have students write poems using the following format to express the meaning of the vocabulary word:

Vocabulary

Adjective, adjective

Verb, verb, verb

Adjective, adjective

Synonym

Each adjective describes the vocabulary word.
Each verb shows the action the vocabulary word exhibits.
The synonym expresses the same idea as the vocabulary word.

ARTISTIC EXPRESSION ACTIVITIES

◆ Billboard design: Have students design billboards using the
definition and understanding of the concept of the vocabulary
word.

COOPERATIVE LEARNING ACTIVITIES

◆ Haiku: Divide the class into groups of four. Each group will
work together to write a poem in haiku style, expressing the
meaning of the vocabulary word.

◆ Haiku is a Japanese poem in three lines of five, seven, and five
syllables, respectively, that presents a clear picture that rouses
emotions. Example:

Courteous students
Are gracious, kind, and polite
To all whom they meet.

Resource C

Learning Styles and Essential Character Discipline

For students who learn from practice:

- Orally and visually present the Student Pledge/Contract and Class Rules.
- Orally and visually present limits, expectations, and consequences.
- Orally and visually present the Essential Character Discipline Vocabulary.
- Ask students the meaning of each word in the Essential Character Discipline Vocabulary.

For students who learn from exploration, ask the following:

- How do you know when a person is _____? (courteous, honest, loyal, showing self-control, showing integrity, showing perseverance, respectful)
- Why is it important to _____? (be courteous, be honest, be loyal, be in control of self, have integrity, show perseverance, be respectful)

For students who learn from exploration and production, ask or have students do the following:

◆ What if all people were *not* _____?
  (courteous, honest, loyal, in control of self, interested in having integrity, trying to have perseverance, respectful)
◆ What if all people were _____?
  (courteous, honest, loyal, in control of self, interested in integrity, showing perseverance, respectful)
◆ Draw a picture expressing the definition of each Essential Character Discipline Vocabulary word.

For students who learn from life experiences, suggest this activity:

◆ Keep a journal of community service projects that fall into each of the Essential Character Discipline Vocabulary categories: courtesy, loyalty, respect, perseverance, honor, integrity, and self-control.

Resource D

*Elements of Essential Character
Discipline: Tools for Teachers*

Rights of Educators

The teacher has the right to

1. Establish a classroom environment that encourages respect for self and others

2. Encourage students to have self-control of their actions to be aware of the wants and needs of self and others

3. Ask for help from parents and the administrators in establishing Essential Character Discipline

Rights of Students

Each student has the right to

1. Learn in an environment that encourages respect and control

2. Have a teacher who will model and encourage behaviors of self-control and respect of self and others

3. Ask for help from parents, teachers, and administrators in developing Essential Character Discipline

Rights of Parents and Guardians

Parents and guardians have the right to

1. Ask for assistance from teachers and principals in developing Essential Character Discipline traits within their children

2. Feel secure in knowing their children's learning environment is a nurturing one that models positive behaviors and academic excellence

Basic Classroom Rules

1. Follow directions.
2. Complete assignments.
3. Work cooperatively with others.
4. Keep self and belongings in personal space.
5. Raise hand to speak in class.

The Essential Character Discipline Teacher

1. Verbally communicates positive behaviors

2. Models positive behaviors

3. Establishes limits and expectations

Essential Character Discipline Vocabulary

1. *Courtesy* is a polite, helpful, or considerate act, remark, or gesture.

2. *Loyalty* is faithfulness to a person, ideal, or cause.

3. *Respect* is feeling or showing honor.

4. *Perseverance* is the act of continuing with a task until it is completed.

5. *Honor* is something done or given for good behavior.

6. *Integrity* is honesty and sincerity.

7. *Self-control* is the regulation of one's emotions and actions.

Expectations for Students

Students are to

1. Be polite to others

2. Be faithful in the completion of academic activities

3. Be considerate of others

4. Do their best to complete all activities

5. Give positive expressions of others

6. Tell the truth

7. Have self-control of their thoughts, words, and actions

Behavioral Objectives

Students will

1. Understand the meaning of the seven words of the Essential Character Discipline Vocabulary (*courtesy, loyalty, respect, perseverance, honor, integrity,* and *self-control*)

2. Voluntarily participate in and model positive classroom behavior

3. Develop a work ethic that leads to academic success

4. Have self-control of actions

5. Orally state the Student Pledge

6. Keep the lines of communication open between parents/guardians and school.

Wanted Positive Behaviors

Courtesy

Saying thank you, please, you're welcome, excuse me, yes, and no

Loyalty

Attending class daily
Completing assignments
Keeping class clean

Respect

Taking turns
Sharing
Listening to others
Using quiet voices

Perseverance

Daily studying
Staying on task

Honor

Paying attention
Following directions
Raising hand to speak

Integrity

Following school and class rules
Telling the truth

Self-Control

No fighting
No using profanity
No stealing
No cheating

Resource E

Student Pledge/Contract

I, _____ , will practice
the positive behavior of integrity. I will show honor for
myself, my teachers, and my fellow students. I will be courteous when dealing with others. I will devote myself to the
completion of my homework and assignments, while practicing perseverance when studying. I will respect myself
and have control of my actions.

_____

(Student's signature)

_____

(Parent's or guardian's signature)

Davis-Johnson, S. P. *Seven Essentials for Character Discipline: Elementary Class-room Management.* Copyright © 2001 by Corwin Press, Inc.

Resource F

Sample Letter to Parents

Dear Parents or Guardians,

I would like to take this opportunity to provide information on Essential Character Discipline. It is important that we establish regular home-school communications. It is my responsibility to keep you informed of the positive behaviors displayed by your child to be successful in academics. Our vocabulary words for the week were: *courtesy, loyalty, respect, perseverance,* and *honor.* These are the first five of the seven Essential Character Discipline Vocabulary foundation words. These words are the cornerstone of Essential Character Discipline. The remaining foundation words are *integrity* and *self-control.* Each day, your child will be introduced to a new Essential Character Discipline Vocabulary word. Please look for weekly notes throughout the school year. I am looking forward to working with you and your child in a positive, successful academic school year.

Sincerely,

Resource G

Sample Award Certificates

ESSENTIAL CHARACTER
DISCIPLINE AWARD

Presented to

_____

for outstanding modeling of

Courtesy

in the classroom

| _____ | _____ |
| Date | Teacher |

ESSENTIAL CHARACTER
DISCIPLINE AWARD

Presented to

_____

for outstanding modeling of

Loyalty

in the classroom

_____   _____

Date   Teacher

ESSENTIAL CHARACTER
DISCIPLINE AWARD

Presented to

_____

for outstanding modeling of

Respect

in the classroom

_____   _____
Date   Teacher

ESSENTIAL CHARACTER DISCIPLINE AWARD

Presented to

_____

for outstanding modeling of

Perseverance

in the classroom

_____	_____
Date	Teacher

ESSENTIAL CHARACTER DISCIPLINE AWARD

Presented to

_____

for outstanding modeling of

Honor

in the classroom

_____   _____
Date   Teacher

ESSENTIAL CHARACTER DISCIPLINE AWARD

Presented to

_____

for outstanding modeling of

Integrity

in the classroom

_____	_____
Date	Teacher

ESSENTIAL CHARACTER DISCIPLINE AWARD

Presented to

_____

for outstanding modeling of

Self-Control

in the classroom

_____   _____
Date   Teacher

Index

CORWIN
PRESS

The Corwin Press logo—a raven striding across an open book—
represents the happy union of courage and learning. We are a pro-
fessional-level publisher of books and journals for K-12 educators,
and we are committed to creating and providing resources that
embody these qualities. Corwin's motto is "Success for All

Printed in the United States
By Bookmasters